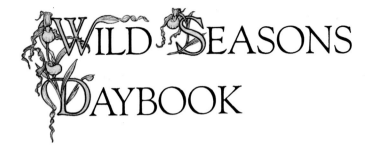

WILD SEASONS DAYBOOK

Best Wishes,
Aleta Karstad.

WILD SEASONS DAYBOOK

Aleta Karstad's Canadian Sketches

Stoddart

0-7737-2254-8

Printed and bound in Hong Kong by
Scanner Art Services, Inc., Toronto

JANUARY

Often the first response we hear to
the lengthening days of winter
is the "Fee-bee" call of the
Chickadee.

Cedar seeds, winter food
for sparrows, Chickadees
and finches.

JANUARY

1

2

3

4

5

Winter wren,
Troglodytes troglodytes
on fir twig

JANUARY

6

_____

7

_____

8

_____

9

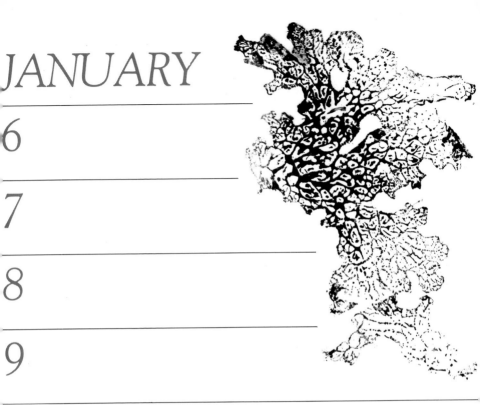

Lobaria pulmonaria
a wet forest treetop lichen

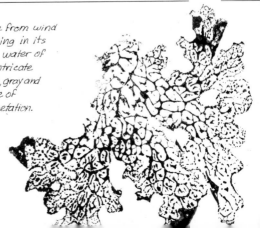

This is the first day we have been free from wind
and rain, nearly continual and amazing in its
violence. I sit on rocks above the water of
the channel, rocks covered with an intricate
tapestry of tiny lichens, salmon, green, gray and
yellow. Bits of moss are stuffing some of
the cracks. To my back is a wall of vegetation.
Vaccinium ovatum is low, with stiff,
glossy, serrate-edged leaves, and
over it lean dead spruces draped
with misty shreds of yellow-
green beard lichen, and young
spruces and cedars crowd
in at the feet of older ones.

JANUARY

10

11

12

13

14

15

16

collected in
early Dec. and
dried indoors

Outdoors in
the cold, they
have turned
brown by
late January.

Winterberry
holly

JANUARY

17

18

19

20

21

22

23

Romano beans

JANUARY

24

25

Watery
berries
of Night-
shade,
mid-winter
food for hungry birds.

26

27

28

29

30

31

JANUARY

21 January 1981   -10°C   Bishops Mills, Ontario

In the late afternoon, the sun is lowering, and the Tree Sparrows have left their feeding here in the old field, but I can see little bird footprints in the snow, one long toe forward, a shorter toe on either side, and one behind. Sometimes a tail-drag shows between the hops. Strings of tracks zig-zag between dry weed seed heads. They trample all about the burr-like avens, and the Evening Primrose, but skirt by a few fluffy, tiny-seeded Goldenrod, as if checking, or pausing to take a few nibbles. Bladder Campion attract a lot of interest. Their smooth, pale golden cups have sides pried off for access to their seeds. From the tracks in the snow and the scattered grey chaff I can see that the sparrows prefer the hairy, brittle Viper's Bugloss, or Blueweed over all the others. Tracks and chaff also show the use of an amazingly delicate, thinly scattered grass. All of these weed seed heads have been out of reach until the last snow fall. As the snow level gets higher, used seed heads are buried, and taller, fresh ones come within the reach of little birds. So too, I noticed, higher willow and apple buds and twigs get nipped off by rabbits. I stop by a fence and a group of tall cedars. The sun has dropped far behind the trees, and from over there a crow calls, wild and defiant. There is no sight or sound of any little birds. They are all safe and sheltered somewhere, preening, fluffing their feathers against the cold of the advancing evening, and turning their wild seed meal into fat to burn as fuel for heat until morning.

Bladder Campion
Silene
vulgaris

Evening Primrose
Oenothera
biennis

Viper's
Bugloss

Echium
vulgare

Rabbit
trimmed
apple branch

FEBRUARY

Scotylidae
sawed off, toothed
elytra

1

2

3

4

Histeridae

clubbed
elbowed
antenna

Sylphidae

5

6

7

FEBRUARY

8

9

10

11

12

13

14

banded antennae
(annuli)

white around eyes

Lycaenidae.

subcosta & R₁,
under posterior
edge of forewing

bulge at base.

Satyridae

forelegs,
reduced greatly

white.

Brush-footed
very reduced
forelegs.
white.

Viceroy,
Nymphalidae.

FEBRUARY

15

16

road-Killed
Screech owl

17

18

19

20

21

oil-Killed
Fulmar

22

FEBRUARY

23

24

25

26

27

28

29

Salix discolor

MARCH

1

2

3

4

5

6

7

MARCH

8

9

10

11

12

13

14

Snow-melt
in the maple bush

A. KARSTAD '82

MARCH

15

16

17

18

19

20

The process of bonding, triggered
by the licking of her wet kid,
was splendid to see, transforming
this skittish yearling into an
attractive and capable mother.

SPRING

Blueberry
in bloom

MARCH

21

22

23

24

25

26

A giant _Equisetum_ sends up stout leafless fruiting bodies first, on scree slopes and road-sides.

As spring warms the black muck of low wet spots, sunshine yellow skunk cabbage rises, vigorous and musky-scented.

MARCH

27

28

29

30

31

Downy
woodpeckers,
studied by
Louise de
Kiriline Law-
rence, are soli-
tary birds, and to
establish enough
trust and cooper-
ation to mate and
nest, require an ela-
borate series of displays
and rituals.

♀ invites
copulation

copulation position is
motionless, and lasts
for 5 to 10 seconds.

♀ in extreme
threat display
toward other
♀

APRIL

1

2

3

4

5

6

7

Bloodroot
Sanguinaria
canadensis

We sliced this root and I
made an orange print with it on my
journal page.

APRIL

SPRING *in the Great Dismal Swamp, Virginia. Flocks of warblers sing in the blossoming trees during the day, and by night the voices of toads and chorus frogs trill and echo through the wooded swamp...The water is clear like black tea, and a warm breeze rustles in the cane along the road.*

Cane,
the native Bamboo
of the eastern U.S.A.

8

9

10

11

APRIL

12

13

14

15

16

17

18

Castor
cana-
densis

Such a difference
between the broad,
softly wrinkled, webbed
hind feet, and the small
fist-like forepaws, so
specially adapted for swim-
ming and holding respectively,
and such a marvelous tail, made of
hard scaly skin over stiff fatty tissue.

APRIL

19

_____

20

_____

21

_____

22

_____

23

_____

24

_____

25

_____

Spring
Beauty,
Clintonia
virginica
from woods
in Stony
Creek,
near
Hamilton
Ontario.
This is the
linear-
leaved
type,
with no
red
stain.

APRIL

breeding male
Pearl Dace

26

27

28

29

30

A. KARSTAD 1979

MAY

Skunk's Misery Campsite:
18 May 1982. At the end of a
short car track of fine grey
dust, a shooting range. But
for mosquitoes, this place is
paradisical. The woods are
thick, moist and deciduous
all around the field — ash, poplar, maple, elm and oaks.
19 May: This morning we noticed a carpenter bee beneath
the gun shelter roof, and big
round nest holes in the rafters.

A. KARSTAD '82

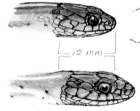

|←12 mm→|

Skunk's Misery snakes

Butlers garter snake: a surprisingly
narrow head for such a blunt profile.
It has a stout body and a very short
tail —— lovely red eye!

Common garter snake is much
lighter and slimmer body, with
a longer nose and broader head
This individual is quite olive.

Crayfish chimneys:
Luther Marsh, Wellington
Co., Ontario. 16 May 1982.
Here I sat and painted the
above-ground evidence of
Onconectes immunis or
Cambarus fodiens. At
night the crustaceans eat
vegetable matter in mea-
dows and ditches, and
spend daylight hours in
the water of their burrows.
The chimneys are made of
balls of soil carried up in
their notched pincers.

MAY

1

2

3

4

5

Primula mistas-sinica

Prim-rose

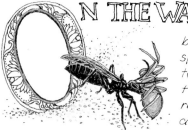

ON THE WAY

We met some digging wasps on an area of sloping sand. One came backwards, very rapidly with a fat brown spider in tow. Such a straight course she took, and such a sensitive abdomen, to sense an obstacle the moment she reached it, even almost to know its size and shape, so deftly she manoevered.

*Arabis
lyrata*

Rock-
cress

10 May
1984

Dorcas
Bay,
Bruce Co.,
Ontario

6

7

8

9

10

11

12

MAY

13

14

15

16

17

18

19

Tamias striatus, as an oatmeal disposal service.

very tiny light tan hairs on cap

smooth area around edge of cap with no tiny 'hairs'

cap is flexible and may be turned inside out, but will spring back.

tan coloured 'hairs'

conical beige-coloured teeth that turn brown after handling

skin of cap is very dark reddish brown

thin layer of same tissue as teeth

very tiny tan hairs as on cap

rather rough brown surface

bark of log

When the groundhog saw our van his demeanor changed to what seemed more characteristic of his kind — on guard.

MAY

20

21

22

23

1 4.9 mm.

This snail is a rich reddish-brown colour and not glossy at all. The growth lines may be a little more numerous than shown.

2. 4.2 mm.

The shell of this snail is light amber or horn coloured, glossy but tending to be corraded a bit on the 'dorsal' or upper surface of the shell. Umbilicus perforate as shown.

3. 3 mm. diam

This whorl is dark because of the body inside.

All these snails had light grey or white bodies (feet). None were black.

This snail is extremely glossy with a shell of dark amber. The dark markings are not on the shell, but on the animal inside. The shell is very thin.

4 3 mm. high

this whorl and the first has no sculpture.

This snail is extremely beautiful, with the ridges very thin and high. When they catch the light they give the otherwise dull shell the look of satin

5 3.4 mm.

This snail looks a little like the one above. it except the shell is white (clear to milky) and there is less depth or relief in the whorls on the 'dorsal' side. The umbilicus is perforate, appearing much like the snail drawn above.

4 Km. n. Louvicourt

Abitibi Co., Quebec. 19 May 1974.

Snails from the vicinity of an old mine. We find higher concentrations of snails near sources of lime, such as this old cement foundation.

6 1.8 mm.

This pupillid has a white lip and one white tooth at the top. Other teeth can hardly be seen inside, with a hand lense. They are the colour of the shell.

The shell is smooth and dark amber (buckwheat honey) coloured

MAY

24

25

26

27

28

29

White crown sparrows, *Zonotrichia leucophrys*, migrate all day about the van, coming through in waves.

Bog rosemary
Andromeda glaucophylla.

Horned lark
Eremophila alpestris

MAY

30

31

Heart shaped leaves of yellow violets cover the ground behind our van, making us direct our steps with care when we walk there. The blossoms are sensitive to all this wind and gloom, opening only to rare brief splashes of sunlight. When this species ripens to seed, the three ovaries are large, pale, and coarsely fuzzy, showing almost as boldly among the dark leaves as the yellow petals had. There are white violets in the woods behind the bog, but less common than the yellow.

Viola pubescens

JUNE

Yellow ladyslipper
*Cypripedium
calceolus*

A. KARSTAD

JUNE

1

2

3

4

5

6

7

Cottongrass
Eriophoum
spissum

from the
Tobermory
Bog

JUNE

8

9

10

11

12

13

14

click
beetle,
*Alaus
oculatus*

Bumble-bee mimic
Hawk-moth:
so bee-like,
it even has
trans-
parent
wings

JUNE

15

16

17

18

19

20

21

Golden ragwort
Senecio aureus

SUMMER

Cypripedium reginae

Blue-eyed grass
Systrinchium montanum

Just a tiny purple
blossom deep inside
the wealth of long grass
and wild riot of meadow
flowers, but its colour,
that of the zenith of
an evening sky,
arrests my gaze
like an eye
in the grass.

on the
other hand,
the rare and special
Showy ladyslippers
can be clearly seen from
the highway, and they have
been nearly all dug up
by vandals.

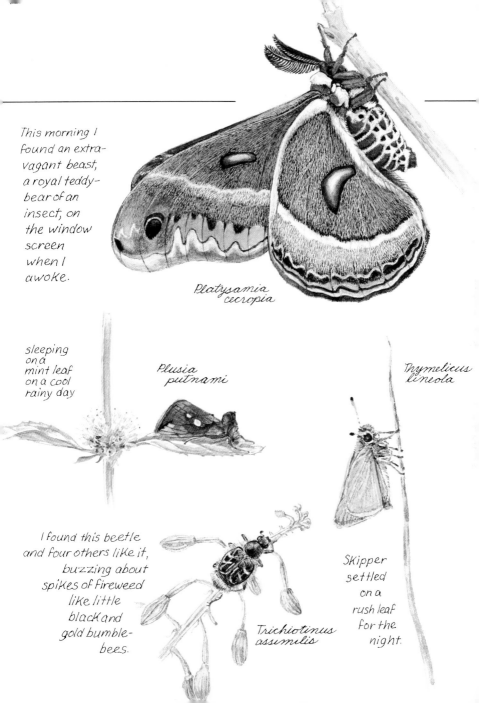

This morning I found an extravagant beast, a royal teddy-bear of an insect, on the window screen when I awoke.

Platysamia cecropia

sleeping on a mint leaf on a cool rainy day

Plusia putnami

Thymelicus lineola

I found this beetle and four others like it, buzzing about spikes of fireweed like little black and gold bumble-bees.

Trichiotinus assimilis

Skipper settled on a rush leaf for the night.

JUNE

22

23

24

25

26

27

Fish fly: This reawakens my
fascination with the forms of
insects. A very strange one, this,
with a serpent-like, long-necked
body, flat head studded ontop
with large simple eyes
and cloaked with large leaf-like
wings, smoky and heavily veined.
The legs are very weak.

As I painted,
the colours faded
at the horizon
until it disappeared,
and the brilliance
grew in the north,
past the left of
my painting,
Finally leaving
the view ahead
of me in tones
of grey.

28

29

30

Luna moth

JULY

Fireweed

Epilobium angustifolium

JULY

1

2

3

Standing in the largest patch of Fireweed,
the air seemed alive with its pinkness,
filling my lungs and casting its
colour on the in-
sides of my eye-
lids. Its aura was
as powerful as
a scent— cool
pink flavour,
with just a whis-
per of the blue
of sky.

JULY

Beach pea
Lathyrus
  japonicus

On my way
out to dig one
of the late-flowering
Indian Paintbrush
in the meadow, I saw constellations
of Water speedwell scattered,
tiny-flowered in pale purple
over damp sand along the fence.
Bees are interested in Yellow
sweet clover now. Little
Skippers are sipping the rich
                    Purple Heal-all.

Painted cup
Castilleja coccinea

JULY

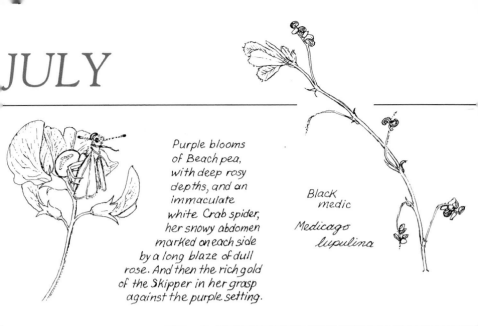

Purple blooms
of Beach pea,
with deep rosy
depths, and an
immaculate
white Crab spider,
her snowy abdomen
marked on each side
by a long blaze of dull
rose. And then the rich gold
of the Skipper in her grasp
against the purple setting.

Black
medic

Medicago
lupulina

4

5

6

The nose of the shrew was very
flexible, and could be turned
at will, up, down or to the side.
This little animal would
turn back toward its tail,
its body bending into a semi-
circle, and the nose would bend too.

Sorex cinereus

JULY

Burrowing owls
Chaplin, Sask.
16 July 1980

On top of a rise, a group of
three stand, outlined by the
late afternoon sun, One hunts
on the hillside beyond them.
It runs a couple of metres,
body held horizontally, then
stops abruptly, flinging its
wings out as it snatches with
its beak at the ground, then
runs, flies for a short distance
and runs again.

7

8

9

10

11

12

13

Horsefly
Hybomitra

Tabanids have eyes like jewelled inlay, but
double-daggered mouthparts, more com-
fortably encountered trapped beneath a
windshield than in their predatory mood
in the open.

Deerfly
Chrysops

14

15

16

17

18

*approach to
Prince Rupert*

JULY

Mantispid Fly
Mantispa interrupta

19

20

21

22

23

24

25

26

Young
Long horned
grasshopper
body 5 mm T

JULY

27

28

28 mm TL.

Elm sawfly,
Cimbex
americana
found
climbing
a birch
stump.
8 July
1984

29

30

31

AUGUST

Helleborine orchid
Epipactis helleborine

AUGUST

Western spotted
frog,
mud-colored above and
geranium pink
beneath.

1

2

3

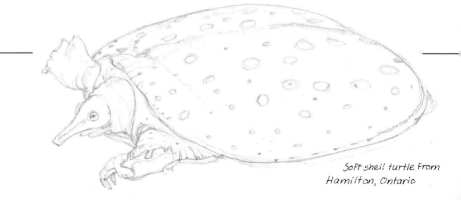

Soft shell turtle from
Hamilton, Ontario

AUGUST

4

5

6

7

8

9

10

*nestling
House sparrow*

AUGUST

11

12

13

From the highway, the Rockies seem
vast, dry and remote. Knife-edged, flat-
planed faces continually reflect the moods
of the sky. On cloudy days they can't be seen,
and on clear days they are
like clouds themselves.

This bush
grew on the bank of
the pond where we watched
the coots yesterday. The stem is
square, bi-colored, light and pithy, and
the leaves are slightly hairy beneath.

Black twin berry
Honeysuckle,
Lonicera
involucrata

AUGUST

14

15

16

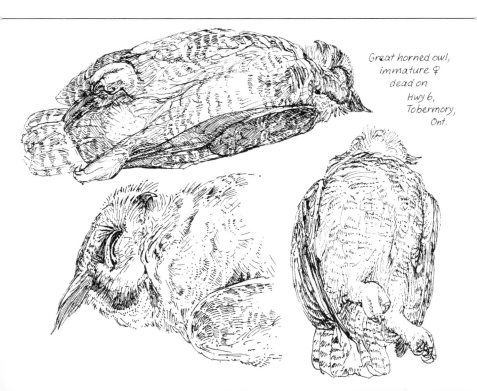

Great horned owl,
immature ♀
dead on
Hwy 6,
Tobermory,
Ont.

AUGUST

*Dog-day
Cicada*

17

18

19

20

21

22

23

*Cord
moss*

*Funaria
hygro-
metrica*

24

*Cross-section
of a lump of
very fine moss, with curly-
stemmed young sporophytes.
The older sporophytes are a
bright rusty colour, and strongly
ridged.*

AUGUST

Michael's Bay, Manitoulin Is.:
The first sand cherry that I've
ever seen, sprawling over
the dunes, with long oval
leaves held vertically,
and soft dark fruit,
the juice of which
is sweet,
and the
tender
skin
sour

Sand cherry
Prunus
susquehanae

25

26

27

AUGUST

28

29

30

31

Bushes of
Ninebark,
raising prickly
clusters of 3-part
fruits, graced the
backs of the sand
dunes, as we returned
to the road through a
moss-floored forest of cedar
and lichen-twigged spruce.

Nine-bark
*Physocarpus
opulifolius*

There is little soil over much of the hard, igneous rock
of the Canadian Sheild.   Lichens and mosses can live on
bare rock because they take their mineral nutrients
from rainfall. Where they trap moisture and erode rock,
cracks fill up with humus, and there, vascular plants can
grow, enriching the terrain and creating microhabitats
which buffer the effects of an extreme climate for
plant and animal life.

SEPTEMBER

A week after I had painted the three views of its chrysalis, we saw a newly emerged Monarch butterfly hanging, motionless beside the empty chrysalis case. Its soft wings hung, gently pleated, straight down, and swayed to the slightest movement of air.

Monarch butterfly
Danaus plexippus

Two weeks ago Fred found this pearly green chrysalis on a dry stick in the fence by our old sandy campsite, where he and Elsa had moved a Monarch caterpillar among various stunted Milkweed plants. The small size of this butterfly may mean that it was our poor thirsty caterpillar.

SEPTEMBER

1

2

3

4

5

6

7

Woodsia fern

SEPTEMBER

5 September 1982

8

9

10

11

Aspen in rock

SEPTEMBER

12

13

14

15

16

17

18

White
Campion

Lychnis
alba

this
segment
of stem
flattened,
and all of
stem
rather
woody.

SEPTEMBER

19

20

21

THERE is a lady-
bird beetle., inside
one of the blossoms
of this Jewelweed,
rocked by a cool breeze from
across the sun sparkling surface of Lake Huron.
I sit on the warm rocks
to paint flowers at
the lapping waters
edge, and hear har-
bour sounds, and
boats, and feel that
Little Tub Harbour
is idyllic.

Jewelweed,

impatiens capensis

AUTUMN

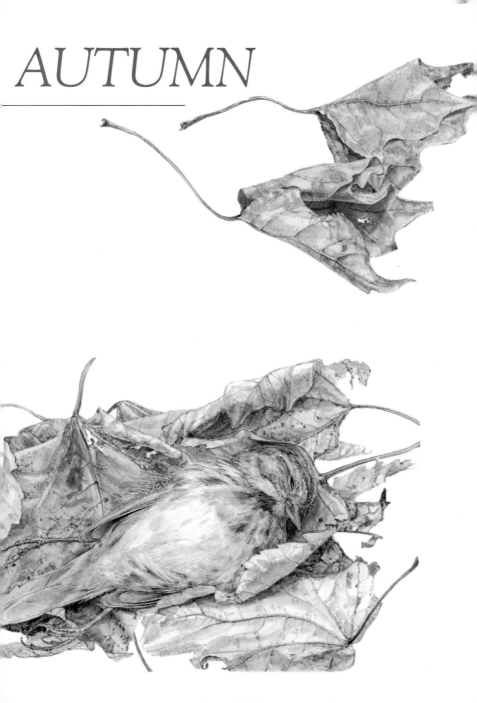

Cepaea
on Tansy:
Cepaea nemo-
ralis is all over
the Bruce Penin-
sula. Walking back
from the docks in the
warm rainy dusk, we
found them in the weedy
areas beside the road,
like carelessly hidden
easter eggs.

SEPTEMBER

22

23

24

25

26

27

Chub whitefish
Coregonus sp.

SEPTEMBER

28

29

30

Triodopsis,
Echo Island

Cranberry, *Vaccinium oxycoccus*

OCTOBER

1

2

3

4

5

6

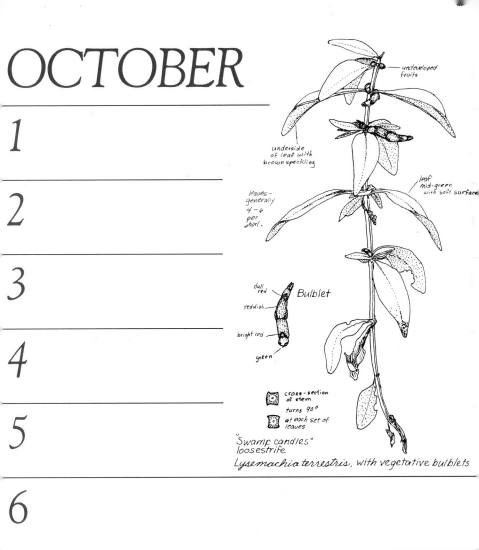

undeveloped fruits

underside of leaf with brown speckling

leaf mid-green with soft surface

leaves - generally 4 - 6 per whorl.

dull red

reddish

bright red

green

Bulblet

cross-section of stem turns 90° at each set of leaves

"Swamp candles"
loosestrife
Lysemachia terrestris, with vegetative bulblets

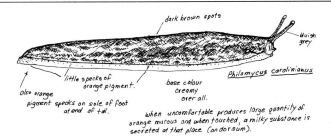

dark brown spots

bluish grey

little specks of orange pigment.

also orange pigment specks on sole of foot at end of tail.

base colour creamy over all.

Philamycus carolinianus

when uncomfortable produces large quantity of orange mucous and when touched, a milky substance is secreted at that place (on dorsum).

So many of the slugs of glaciated North America are introduced that it is a comfort to find one of these big native mushroom-eating slugs.

OCTOBER

7

8

9

10

14 October 1973
I have drawn a soap-
wort gentian
growing where we
camped 3 miles
n. e. of Smyrna,
Delaware, U.S.A.
It is of a lighter
blue than G.
Autumnalis
and its blooms do
not open as wide.
As we recorded the calls
of Canada geese we watched
the corkscrewing motion of
geese coming down to land on
the water. Some individuals flew
upside down for a moment. The
weather was cool and windy.

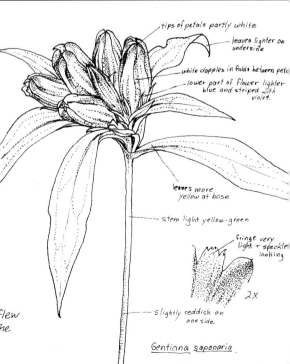

tips of petals partly white

leaves lighter on
underside

white dapples in folds between peta

lower part of flower lighter
blue and striped with
violet.

leaves more
yellow at base

stem light yellow-green

fringe very
light + speckle
looking

2x

slightly reddish on
one side

Gentiana saponaria

OCTOBER

11

12

dorsal view

ventral view

White poplar

13

14

15

Young puffball

16

Zonitoides sp. land snail

In our Toronto Islands collection there were no two-toned specimens, but this drawing is diagramatic, to show the normal dark color of the population, and the light tan color of the individual found.

OCTOBER

17

18

19

20

the
Freshwater
clam,
Lampsilis radiata

21

This young catfish
has one forked whisker,
probably the result of ab-
normal regrowth after injury.
Are catfish whiskers spine-
mimics as well as sensory organs?
Perhaps they look agressive to one
who has been pricked
by a dorsal spine.

22

23

*Ictalurus
nebulosus*

24

OCTOBER

25

26

27

28

29

30

31

Rabbits
Foot
Clover

Trifolium arvense

NOVEMBER

Moonrise over the Catskills

A. KARSTAD '80

NOVEMBER

1

2

3

4

5

6

7

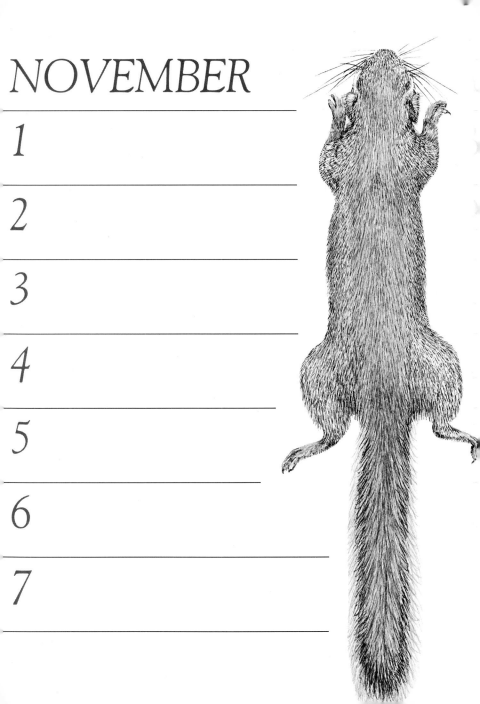

NOVEMBER

8

9

10

11

12

13

Sassafrass
albidum

Red squirrel
Tamiasciurus hudsonicus
Saucy busybody of the cedartops,
I revel in your bright carrotty colour,
and am amazed to hear that the brightest
part of it is water-soluble.

NOVEMBER

14

15

16

17

18

19

20

Atriplex sp. from West Haven Beach, Conn. Within the beach there are patches of salt marsh conditions, rather unstable but with mud snails and both *Spartina* grasses.

Selaginella apoda — a vascular plant living like a moss — a delicate translucent tracery, on the bank of Sandy Pond, Lincoln, Mass.   17 Nov. 1978

Ruffed grouse
Bonasa umbellus

21

22

23

NOVEMBER

24

25

26

27

28

29

30

A. KARSTAD 1975

DECEMBER

DECEMBER

1

2

3

4

5

In early December many
stream animals are moving
from banks and shallows
into deeper water.
They will only survive
where the water does
not freeze to the
bottom and is not
wholly sealed off
from oxygen by ice.

Mink Frog
*Rana
septentrionalis*

DECEMBER

6

7

8

9

10

Northern
crayfish
Orconectes virilis

DECEMBER

Wild cucumber
Echinocystis lobata

11

12

13

14

15

16

DECEMBER

17

18

19

20

21

Wild cucumber drapes the cedars and rail fences with voiceless bells of prickly straw colored filigree.

Some still contain large hard-shelled seeds.

WINTER

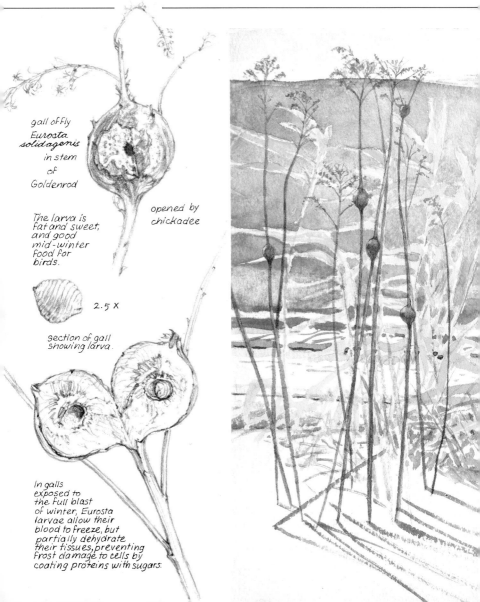

gall of fly
*Eurosta
solidagenis*
in stem
of
Goldenrod

opened by
chickadee

The larva is
fat and sweet,
and good
mid-winter
food for
birds.

2.5 X

section of gall
showing larva.

In galls
exposed to
the full blast
of winter, Eurosta
larvae allow their
blood to freeze, but
partially dehydrate
their tissues, preventing
frost damage to cells by
coating proteins with sugars.

DECEMBER

22

23

24

25

26

27

28

DECEMBER

29

30

31

Poinsettia, a tropical *Euphorbia*,
has clusters of small, red-anthered
flowers equipped with external cups
for nectar droplets to attract pollinators,
all set about with large red bracts.

AFTERWORD

As the *Wild Seasons Daybook* goes to press, thirteen years of my journals are unbound, and I am sending the pages off with many other unpublished paintings and drawings. Seldom in all these years have I not had my current journal on hand to bring friends up-to-date with our travels and discoveries or to show and explain the entries to anyone interested in the nature of my art and my involvement with natural history.

I don't write in my journals every day. I could well use that discipline, but to avoid having pages bare of illustration I usually write only when I also have time to draw. So most often the drawing or watercolour comes first, and the text is written around it.

My first journals, as I was taught by Franklin D. Ross, were detailed records of all my natural history observations, both informed and naive, written in ruled volumes, and illustrated only occasionally with ink sketches. But through the years the journals seemed to set their own standards and to demand ever more illustration. Each time as I portray a bit of the natural world I am amazed at the gradual way in which form and beauty come to notice. My responsibility for the truth of the image teaches me so much more than less reconstructive methods of observation could. I have found that to draw is to learn, and I intend to keep on learning.

When I work in my journal I feel the satisfaction of possession, since there is no possibility of the work being given away or sold—the eventual fate of everything done on separate paper, no matter how great the sentimental attachment. Some such separate works have come back for this book, and I thank Mr. and Mrs. Donald C. O'Brien, Phil and Mary Wright, Mr. and Mrs. H. Weller, Larry and Anstice Esmonde-White, and the Rising family for the loan of paintings reproduced

AFTERWORD

here. The staff at Methuen have been patient and understanding in their careful assembly of the myriad bits of lettering and artwork. Botanists at the National Museum of Natural Sciences and entomologists at Agriculture Canada were tremendously helpful in identifying the subjects of drawings, especially Dr. Monty Wood. Also to be thanked are all the friends who have encouraged my journal keeping over the years, especially Robin Brass, dear Jess, Karen Tousaw, Francis and Joyce Cook, my sister Karen, and my parents. My daughter, Elsa, has endured many days of less-than-maternal attention during the work of preparation, and my biologist husband, Fred Schueler, friend, teacher, and travelling companion, has been invaluable at every stage of the planning, selection, identification, and preparation of artwork and text.

I look forward to having this collection of many journal pages and pieces in my hand as one little book. And I look forward especially to the satisfaction of letting everyone write their own thoughts, dates, and records in my *Wild Seasons Daybook* and so perhaps encouraging them to write and draw in journals of their own.

Bishops Mills,
Ontario
January 1985

NOTES

NOTES

NOTES

LIST OF NAMES, DATES, LOCALITIES, AND MEDIA FOR ILLUSTRATIONS

Illustrations are listed by month and page, and "watercolour" is abbreviated to "wc."

FRONT COVER. Eastern chipmunk, *Tamias striatus*, Jun '80, Bishops Mills, Grenville Co., Ont., wc, coll. of Larry and Anstice Esmonde-White. FRONTISPIECE. Sedge and primrose, *Carex richardsonii* and *Primula mistassinica*, May '84, Baptist Harbour, Bruce Peninsula, Ont., wc, coll. of Mr. and Mrs. H. Weller. TITLE PAGE. Yellow warbler, *Dendroica petechia*, Aug '84, Avenley, Ont., wc. REGISTRATION PAGE. White-tailed deer antler, *Odocoileus virginianus*, Jun '76, Killbear Park, Ont., ink.

JANUARY. 5: Chickadee and cedar, *Parus atricapillus* and *Thuja occidentalis*, Jan. '85, Bishops Mills, Ont., wc. 6: Winter wren, *Troglodytes troglodytes*, Dec '76, 4 km E Qualicum Beach, Vancouver I., B.C., wc. 7: Lichen, *Lobaria pulmonaria*, Feb '77, Tofino, Vancouver I., B.C., acrylic print. 8: Winterberry holly, *Ilex verticillata*, dried, Dec '84; fresh, Jan '85; Bishops Mills, Ont., ink and wc. 9: Red squirrel, *Tamiasciurus hudsonicus*, Jan '80, Pimisi Bay, Renfrew Co., Ont., ink. Romano beans, *Phaseolus vulgaris*, Jan '74, Kensington Market, Toronto, Ont., ink. 10: Nightshade berries, *Solanum dulcamara*, Jan '85, Bishops Mills, Ont., wc. 11: Bladder campion, evening primrose, viper's bugloss, and apple, *Silene vulgaris*, *Oenothera biennis*, *Echium vulgare*, and *Pyrus malus*, Jan '81, Bishops Mills, Ont., ink and wc.

FEBRUARY. 12: Beetles, Coleoptera, Feb '81, Carleton University collection, ink. 13: Butterflies, Lepidoptera, Feb. '81, Carleton University collection, ink. 14: Screech owl talons, *Otus asio*, Feb '81, Merrickville, Ont., ink. Fulmar, *Fulmarus glacialis*, Apr '77, Long Beach, Vancouver I., B.C., ink.

15: Pussywillow, *Salix discolor*, Feb '84, Bishops Mills, Ont., wc.

MARCH. 16: Snails and maple keys, *Cepaea nemoralis* and *Acer negundo*, 1974, Rockwood, Ont., wc, coll. of James and Trudy Rising. 17: Leaf in snow, *Acer saccharum*, Mar '82, Bishops Mills, Ont., wc. 18: Nubian goats, *Capra hircus*, Mar '83, Bishops Mills, Ont., ink. 19: Blueberry in bloom, *Vaccinium angustifolium*, Jun '84, Tobermory Bog, Bruce Peninsula, Ont., wc. 20: Western skunk cabbage and horsetail, *Lysichiton kamtschatcense* and *Equisitum telmateia*, Apr '77, Long Beach, Vancouver I., B.C., ink. 21: Downy woodpecker, *Picoides pubescens*, 1984, ink.

APRIL. 22: Bloodroot, *Sanguinaria canadensis*, Apr '80, 14 km NNE Mt. Union, Pa., ink and wc. 23: Cane, *Arundinaria tecta*, Apr '80, Great Dismal Swamp, Va., ink and wc. 24: Beaver, *Castor canadensis*, Apr '83, Bishops Mills, Ont., ink. 25: Spring beauty, *Claytonia virginica*, Apr '83, Stoney Creek, Hamilton-Wentworth Region, Ont., ink. Spring beauty, *Claytonia caroliniana*; trout lily and dead leaves, *Erythronium americanum*, *Quercus*, and *Ostrya virginiana*; Apr '83, Port Robinson, Ont., ink and wc. 26: Pearl dace, *Semotilus margarita*, Apr '83, Luther Marsh, Wellington Co., Ont., ink and wc. Swamp landscape, May '79, 5 km S North Gower, Ont., wc.

MAY. 27: Rifle range landscape (wc); Butler's and common garter snakes, *Thamnophis butleri* and *T. sirtalis* (ink and wc); May '82, Skunk's Misery, 4 km ENE Bothwell, Ont. Crayfish chimney, May '82, Luther Marsh, Wellington Co., Ont., wc. 28: Primrose, *Primula mistassinica*, May '84, Dorcas Bay, Bruce Peninsula, Ont., ink and wc. Pompilid wasp and spider, May '84, Carson L. Park, Renfrew Co., Ont., ink and wc. 29: Rock cress, *Arabis lyrata*, May

'84, Dorcas Bay, Bruce Peninsula, Ont., ink and wc. 30: Eastern chipmunk, *Tamias striatus*; mushroom, *Auriscalpium vulgare*; May '74, 4 km N Louvicourt, Abitibi Co., Que., ink. Woodchuck, *Marmota monax*, May '84, Cabot Head, Bruce Peninsula, Ont., ink. 31: Snails: 1. *Discus sp.*, 2. *Zonitoides arboreus*, 3. *Euconulus fulvus*, 4. *Zoogenetes harpa*, 5. *Retinella binneyana*, 6. poss. *Vertigo sp.*, May '74, 4 km N Louvicourt, Abitibi Co., Que., ink. 32: Whitecrown sparrows, *Zonotrichia leucophrys*, May '84, Cabot Head, Bruce Peninsula, Ont., wc. Horned lark, *Eremophila alpestris*, May '74; bog rosemary, *Andromeda glaucophylla*, May '74; 52 km SW Matagami, Que., wc. 33: Yellow violet, *Viola pubescens*, May '84, Tobermory, Ont., wc.

JUNE. 34: Yellow lady's slipper, *Cypripedium calceolus*, Jun '84, Tobermory, Ont., wc. 35: Cottongrass, *Eriophorum spissum*, Jun '84, Tobermory Bog, Ont., wc. 36: Click beetle, *Alaus oculatus*, Jun '78, breakwater, Long Point, Norfolk Co., Ont., wc. Snowberry clearwing, *Hemaris diffinis*, Jun '79, 6 km E Havelock, Ont., ink and wc. 37: Golden ragwort, *Senecio aureus*, Jun '80, Bishops Mills, Ont., ink. 38: Blue-eyed grass, *Sisyrinchium montanum*, Jul '84; showy lady's slipper, *Cypripedium reginae*, Jul '84; Tobermory, Ont., wc, coll. of Mr. and Mrs. Donald C. O'Brien. 39: Cecropia moth, *Platysamia cecropia*, Jun '78, Backus Woods, Norfolk Co., Ont., wc. Moth on mint, *Plusia putnami* and *Mentha*, Jul '80, Kasiks and Skeena rivers, B.C., wc. Scarab beetle on fireweed, *Trichiotinus assimilis* and *Epilobium angustifolium*, Jul '84, Tobermory Bog, Ont., wc. European skipper, *Thymelicus lineola*, Jul '84, Tobermory, Ont., wc. 40: Fish fly, *Chauliodes rasticornis*, Jun '84, 4 km SW Cape Chin North, Bruce Peninsula, Ont., wc. 41: Georgian Bay at sunset, Jun '84, Cape Chin South, Bruce Peninsula, Ont.,

wc. Luna moth, *Actias luna*, Jun '84, Tobermory, Ont., wc.

JULY. 42–43: Fireweed, *Epilobium angustifolium*, Jul '84, Tobermory, Ont., wc. 44: Beach pea, *Lathyrus japonica*, Jul '84; painted cup, *Castilleja coccinea*, Jul '84; Tobermory, Ont., wc, coll. of Mr. and Mrs. Donald C. O'Brien. 45: Crab spider with skipper on beach pea, Jul '84, Dunks Bay, Bruce Peninsula, Ont., ink. Black medic, *Medicago lupulina*, Jul '81, Bishops Mills, Ont., ink. Shrew, *Sorex cinereus*, Jul '74, Speed R., NW Oustic, Wellington Co., Ont., wc. 46: Burrowing owls, *Speotyto cunicularia*, Jul '80, E of Chaplin, Sask., ink. Deer fly and horse fly, *Chrysops* and *Hybomitra*, Jul '80, 30 km NW Campbell River, Vancouver I., B.C., wc. 47: Approach to Prince Rupert, B.C., by ferry, Jul '80, ink. 48: Mantispid fly, *Mantispa interrupta*, Jul '80, S of Almonte, Ont., ink and wc. Young long-horned grasshopper, *Tettigoniidae*, Jul '78, Brookfield, Conn., ink and wc. 49: Elm sawfly, *Cimbex americana*, Jul '84, Warner Point, Bruce Peninsula, Ont., ink and wc.

AUGUST. 50: Helleborine orchid, *Epipactis helleborine*, Aug '84, Tobermory, Ont., wc. 51: Western spotted frog, *Rana pretiosa*, Aug '80, Moricetown, B.C., pencil. Spiny softshell turtle, *Trionyx spiniferus* (in captivity), Aug '82, Hamilton Harbour, Ont., pencil. 52: Coots, *Fulica americana*, Aug '80, Topley, B.C., ink. Nestling house sparrow, *Passer domesticus*, Aug '81, Oxford Mills, Ont., ink. 53: Black twinberry honeysuckle, *Lonicera involucrata*, Aug '80, Topley, B.C., ink and wc. Mountains, Aug '80, Holmes R., SE of McBride, B.C., ink. 54: Great horned owl, *Bubo virginianus*, Aug '84, Tobermory, Ont., ink. 55: Dog-day cicada, *Tibicen pruinosa*, Aug '71, Warren Dunes, Lake Michigan, Mich., ink. Cord moss, *Funaria hygrometrica*, Aug '80, 19 km NW

Pembina R., Forestry Trunk Rd., Alta., ink. 56–57: Sand cherry, *Prunus susquehanae*; ninebark, *Physocarpus opulifolius*; Aug '84, Michaels Bay, Manitoulin I., Ont., ink and wc.

SEPTEMBER. 58: Rock scene, *Woodsia* fern, *Cladonia* lichen, Sep '82, Kenoji L., Thunder Bay dist., Ont., oil, for coll. of Bruce Hyer. 59: Monarch butterfly, *Danaus plexippus*, Sep '84, Tobermory, Ont., wc and pencil. 60: *Woodsia* fern, prob. *W. ilvestris*, Sep '82, Thunder Bay, Ont., ink. 61: Cabin, Sep '82; aspen, *Populus tremuloides*, Sep '82; Wabikini L., Thunder Bay dist., Ont., ink. 62: White campion, *Lychnis alba*, Sep '83, Midhurst, Ont., ink and wc. 63: Jewelweed, *Impatiens capensis*, Sep '83, Tobermory, Ont., ink and wc. 64: Song sparrow and maple leaves, *Zonotrichia melodia* and *Acer saccharum*, Oct. '83, Bishops Mills, Ont., wc, coll. of Phil and Mary Wright. 65: Snail on tansy, *Cepaea nemoralis* and *Tanacetum vulgare*, Sep '83, Tobermory, Ont., wc, coll. of Phil and Mary Wright. 66: Massasauga rattlesnake, *Sistrurus catenatus*, Sep '83, Cameron L., Bruce Peninsula, Ont., ink and wc. Chub whitefish, *Coregonus cf. artedii*, Sep '83, Lake Huron near Tobermory, Ont., ink and wc. 67: Snail shell, *Triodopsis*, Echo I.; cranberry, *Vaccinium oxycoccus*, Cove I.; Sep '83, Tobermory Is., Ont., ink and wc.

OCTOBER. 68: Swamp candles, *Lysimachia terrestris*, Oct '73, 5 km S Chatsworth, N.J., ink. Slug, *Philomycus carolinianus*, Oct '73, 11.5 km W, 6 km N, Chatsworth, N.J., ink. 69: Soapwort gentian, *Gentiana saponaria*, Oct '73, 5 km NE Smyrna, Del., ink. 70: White poplar leaves, *Populus alba* (ink); puffball, *Bovista cf. plumosa* (tinted ink); Oct '73, High Park, Toronto, Ont. Snail shell, *Zoni-*

toides, Oct '73, Centre I., Toronto, Ont., tinted ink. 71: Lamp mussel, *Lampsilis radiata*, Oct '73, Oneida L., New York, ink. Brown bullhead, *Ictalurus nebulosus*, Oct '73, 25 km E Belleville, Ont., pencil. 72: Rabbit's-foot clover, *Trifolium arvense*, Oct '84, Victoria Beach, N.B., wc.

NOVEMBER. 73: Rising moon, Nov '79, Catskill Mtns., near Roscoe, New York, wc. 74–75: Red squirrel, *Tamiasciurus hudsonicus*, Nov '74, Speed R., NW Oustic, Wellington Co., Ont., coloured inks. 75: Sassafras twig, *Sassafras albidum*, Nov '78, Stoney Brook, Long I., New York, wc. 76: Saltwort, *Atriplex sp.*, Nov '78, West Haven, Conn., ink and wc. Spikemoss, *Selaginella apoda*, Nov '78, Sandy Pond, Lincoln, Mass., ink. 77: Ruffed grouse, *Bonasa umbellus*, Nov '78, Athol, Franklin Co., Mass., ink and wc. 78: House mouse, *Mus musculus*, Nov '73, Toronto, Ont., pencil.

DECEMBER. 79: Kemptville Creek, Dec '84, 3 km N Bishops Mills, Ont., wc. 80: Mink frog, *Rana septentrionalis*, fall '82, Gatineau Park, Que., wc. 81: Crayfish, *Orconectes virilis*, Dec '84, Oxford Mills, Ont., wc. 82–83: Wild cucumber, *Echinocystis lobata*, Dec '84, Bishops Mills, Ont., ink. 84–85: Goldenrod and goldenrod gallfly, *Solidago* and *Eurosta solidagenis*; details, Jan '85, Bishops Mills, Ont., pencil; scene, Feb '82, Oxford Station, Grenville Co., Ont., wc. 87: Poinsettia, *Euphorbia pulcherrima*, Jan '85, Kemptville, Ont., wc. 93: Herb Robert, *Geranium robertianum*, Sep '83, Tobermory, Ont., wc. 96: White trillium, *Trillium grandiflorum*, May '82, Highland Glen Conservation Area, Ont., wc.

BACK COVER. Pincherry, *Prunus pensylvanica*, Aug '84, Tobermory, Ont., wc.